ME AND THE MEASURE OF THINGS

ME AND THE MEASURE OF THINGS

by Joan Sweeney   illustrated by Annette Cable

Dell Dragonfly Books New York

For Devan, Tegan, and their Uncle Bill
—J.S.

To all the kids big and little. We can all measure up.
Keep learning!
—A.C.

Published by
Dell Dragonfly Books
an imprint of
Random House Children's Books
a division of Random House, Inc.
1540 Broadway
New York, New York 10036

Text copyright © 2001 by Joan Sweeney
Illustrations copyright © 2001 by Annette Cable

Visit us on the Web! www.randomhouse.com/kids
Educators and librarians, for a variety of teaching tools, visit us at www.randomhouse.com/teachers

Library of Congress Cataloging-in-Publication Data
Sweeney, Joan, 1930–
Me and the measure of things / by Joan Sweeney ; illustrated by Annette Cable.
p. cm.
ISBN: 0-375-81101-X (trade) 0-375-91101-4 (lib. bdg.) 0-440-41756-2 (pbk.)
1. Mensuration—Juvenile literature 2. Weights and measures—Juvenile literature [1. Weights and Measures.]
I. Cable, Annette, ill. II. Title.
QA465 .S84 2001
530.8—dc21   00-067775

Reprinted by arrangement with Crown Publishers

Printed in the United States of America

September 2002

10 9 8 7 6 5 4 3 2 1

This is me on the day I was born.

I weighed seven pounds and measured 20 inches long.

This is me today. I weigh 52 pounds—and
I measure 48 inches tall.

Whenever I want to know the size of something—how much it weighs, how long it is—I figure it out with weights and measures.

How much?

How much baking mix do I need for pancakes?

How many ounces of Gummi Bears are there in a bagful?

How many?

How far?

How far is the farmers' market from my house?

Weights and measures tell me how much, how many, how heavy, how tall, and how far.

To measure dry things, I use special spoons and cups. This is a **teaspoon**. There are three teaspoons in one **tablespoon**. There are 16 tablespoons in one **cup**. And I need two cups of baking mix to make pancakes.

1 teaspoon

3 teaspoons = 1 Tablespoon

I also need one cup of milk. But to measure liquids, I use ounces, cups, pints, quarts, and gallons.

I drink eight **ounces** of juice every morning.
That's the same as one **cup**.

8 ounces =
1 cup

When my brother drinks a cup of juice, too, our two cups equal one **pint**. And if we pour enough juice for my whole family, we pour four cups, or two pints. That's one **quart** of juice. And four quarts equal one **gallon**—enough to fill my watering can to the top. With water, not juice!

4 quarts = 1 gallon

1 ounce

At the candy store, they weigh things on a scale. One **ounce** of Gummi Bears can fit in the palm of my hand.

Sixteen ounces of Gummi Bears equal one **pound**—
a whole bagful.

16 ounces =
1 pound

And 2,000 pounds of Gummi Bears are the same as one **ton**. Enough for every kid in my town!

2,000 pounds = 1 <u>ton</u>

Suppose I want to figure out how long something is. This postage stamp measures one **inch**. Twelve inches are the same as one **foot**, the length of my ruler. Three feet equal one **yard**— enough paper to draw a big poster. That's one foot shorter than me!

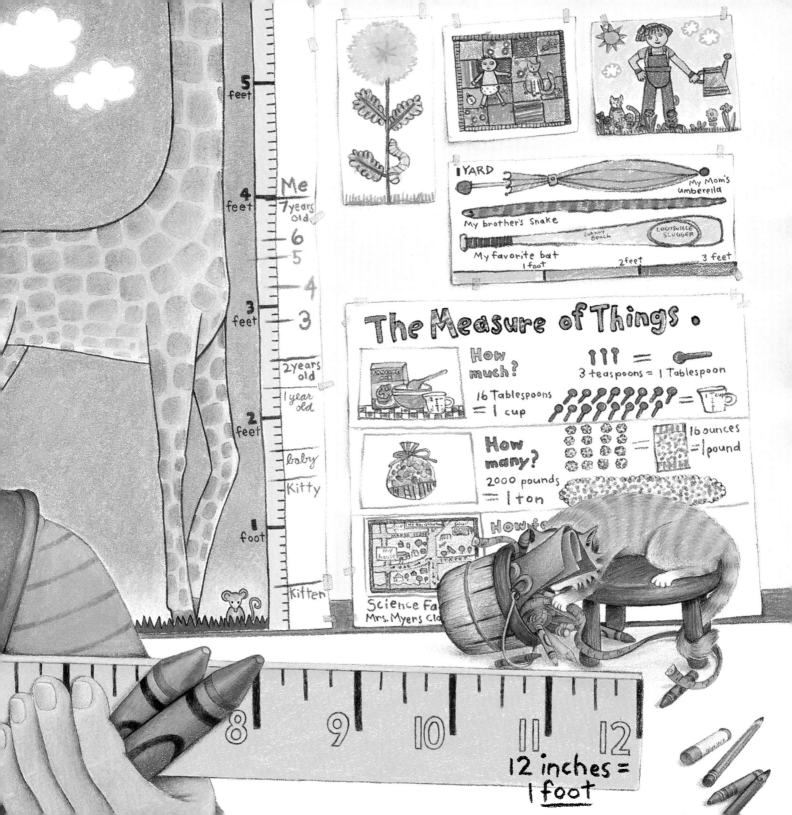

And 5,280 feet are the same as one **mile**. That's how far the farmers' market is from my house.

5,280 feet = 1 mile

At the farmers' market, they use boxes and baskets to measure. We buy one **pint** of strawberries. We buy one **quart** of plums—the same as two pints.

2 pints=
1quart

4 pecks = 1 bushel

8 quarts = 1 peck

We buy one **peck** of potatoes—the same as eight quarts. And we buy one **bushel** of apples—the same as four pecks.

It's easy to see why weights and measures play an important part in our lives. Every day we use them to size things up!

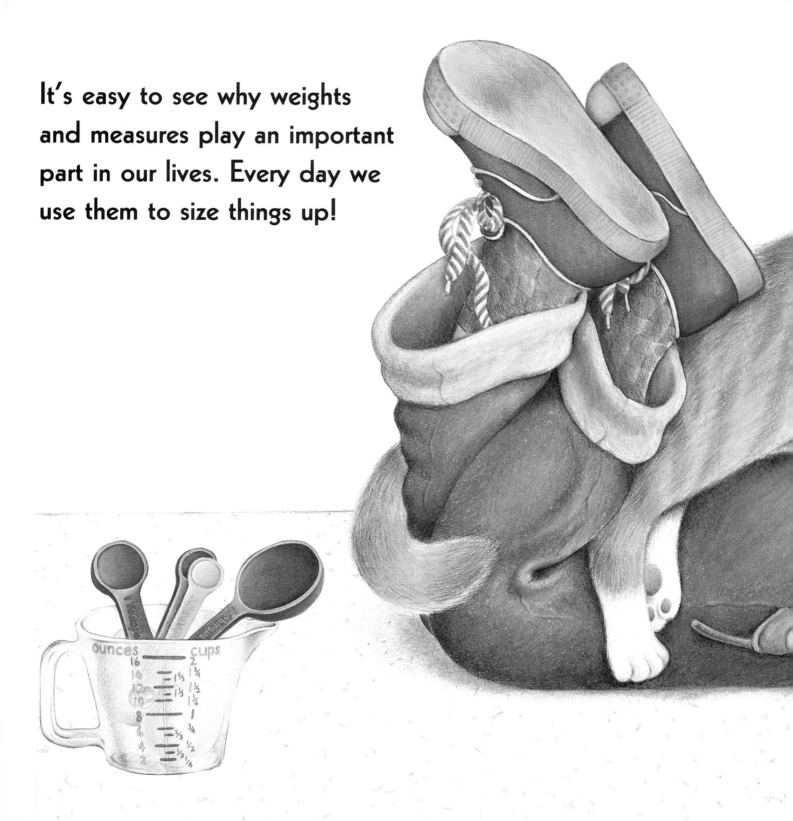

The Measure of Things

3 teaspoons = 1 Tablespoon

16 Tablespoons = 1 cup

1 cup

8 ounces = 1 cup

2 cups = 1 pint

2 pints = 1 quart

4 quarts = 1 gallon

16 ounces = 1 pound

2000 pounds = 1 ton

12 inches = 1 foot

3 feet = 1 yard

5,280 feet = 1 mile

2 pints = 1 quart

8 quarts = 1 peck

4 pecks = 1 bushel

J   15.95
530.8
S

Sweeney, Joan

Me and the Measure of Things